The T♥ddler's handb👁👁k

With over 100 Words that every kid should know

BY DAYNA MARTIN

INGLÊS/PORTUGUÊS

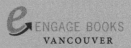

ENGAGE BOOKS
VANCOUVER

1

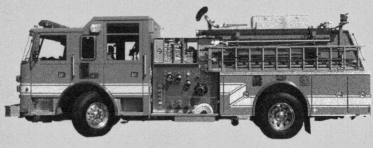

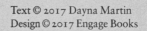

eENGAGE BOOKS

Mailing address
PO BOX 4608
Main Station Terminal
349 West Georgia Street
Vancouver, BC
Canada, V6B 4A1

www.engagebooks.ca

Written & compiled by: Dayna Martin
Edited & translated by: A.R. Roumanis
Proofread by: Anita Faria
Designed by: A.R. Roumanis
Photos supplied by: Shutterstock
Photo on page 47 by: Faye Cornish

FIRST EDITION / FIRST PRINTING

LIBRARY AND ARCHIVES CANADA CATALOGUING IN PUBLICATION

Martin, Dayna, 1983–, author
    The toddler's handbook : numbers, colors, shapes, sizes, ABC animals, opposites, and sounds, with over 100 words that every kid should know / written by Dayna Martin ; edited by A.R. Roumanis.

Issued in print and electronic formats.
Text in English and Portuguese.
ISBN 978-1-77226-458-6 (bound). –
ISBN 978-1-77226-459-3 (paperback). –
ISBN 978-1-77226-460-9 (pdf). –
ISBN 978-1-77226-461-6 (epub). –
ISBN 978-1-77226-461-6 (kindle)

1. Portuguese language – Vocabulary – Juvenile literature.
2. Vocabulary – Juvenile literature.
3. Word recognition – Juvenile literature.
I. Martin, Dayna, 1983– . Toddler's handbook.
II. Martin, Dayna, 1983– . Toddler's handbook. Portuguese.
III. Title.

PC5256.M37 2017   J469'.81   C2017-905768-5
                                       C2017-905769-3

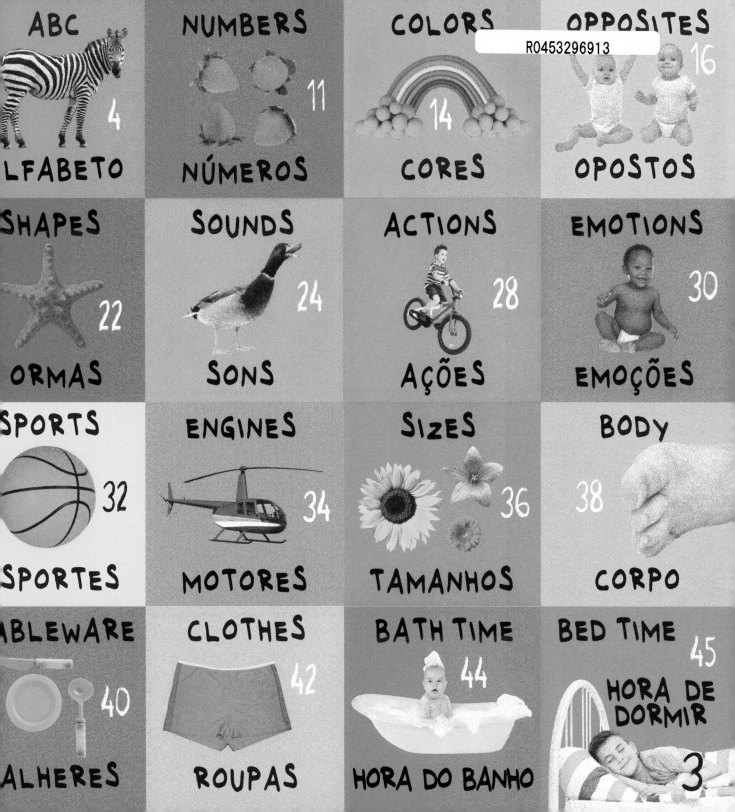

ABC
4
LFABETO

NUMBERS
11
NÚMEROS

COLORS
14
CORES

OPPOSITES
16
OPOSTOS

SHAPES
22
ORMAS

SOUNDS
24
SONS

ACTIONS
28
AÇÕES

EMOTIONS
30
EMOÇÕES

SPORTS
32
SPORTES

ENGINES
34
MOTORES

SIZES
36
TAMANHOS

BODY
38
CORPO

BLEWARE
40
ALHERES

CLOTHES
42
ROUPAS

BATH TIME
44
HORA DO BANHO

BED TIME
45
HORA DE DORMIR
3

Aa Alligator

Jacaré

Bear

Bb

Urso

Cat

Cc

Gato

4

Dog

Dd

Cachorro

Elephant

Ee

Elefante

Fox

Ff

Raposa

Goat

Gg

Cabra

5

Horse

Hh

Cavalo

Iguana

Ii

Iguana

Jaguar

Jj

Jaguar

6

Koala

Kk

Coala

Lion

Ll

Leão

Mouse

Mm

Rato

Newt

Nn

Tritão

Otter

Oo
Lontra

Pig

Pp
Porco

Quail

Qq
8 Codorniz

Rabbit

Rr
Coelho

Seal

Ss

Foca

Tiger

Tt

Tigre

Uakari

Uu

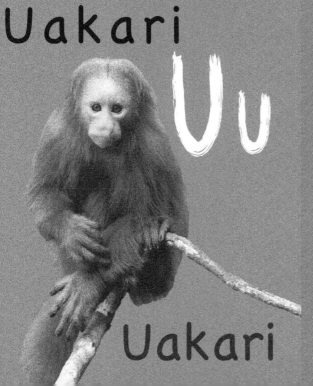

Uakari

Vulture

Vv

Abutre 9

Weasel

Ww

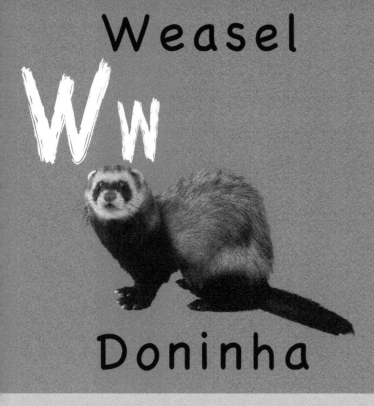

Doninha

X-ray fish

Xx

Peixe raio x

Yak

Yy

10   Iaque

Zebra

Zz

Zebra

Apple

One
1
Uma

Maçã

Crackers

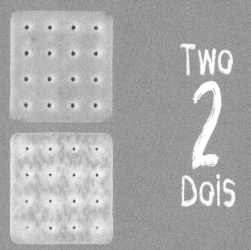

Two
2
Dois

Bolachas

Watermelon slices

Three
3
Três

Fatias de fruta

11

Strawberries

Four
4
Quatro

Morangos

Carrots

Five
5
Cinco

Cenouras

Tomatoes

Six
6
Seis

12

Tomates

Pumpkins

Seven
7
Sete

Abóboras

Fruit slices

Eight
8
Oito

Fatias de frutas

Potatoes

Nine
9
Nove

Batatas

Cookies

Ten
10
Dez

Biscoitos 13

Rainbow

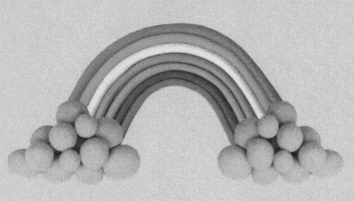

Arco Íris

Red

Vermelho

Orange

14 Laranja

Yellow

Amarelo

Green

Verde

Blue

Azul

Indigo

Índigo

Violet

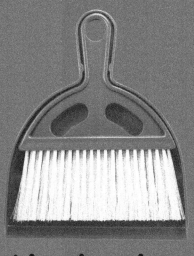

Violeta 15

Up

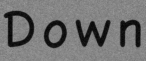

Cima

Down

Baixo

In

16 # Dentro

Out

Fora

Hot

Quente

Cold

Frio

Wet

Molhado

Dry

Seco

Front

De frente

Back

De trás

On

Ligado

18

Off

Desligado

Open

Aberto

Closed

Fechado

Empty

Vazio

Full

Cheio

19

Safe

Seguro

Dangerous

Perigoso

Big

Small

Grande

Pequeno

Asleep
Adormecido

Awake

Acordado

Long

Longo

Short

Curto 21

Circle

Círculo

Square

Quadrado

Triangle

22 Triângulo

Rectangle

Retângulo

Diamond

Diamante

Star

Estrela

Oval

Oval

Heart

Coração

23

Sneeze

Ah-choo

Atchô

Espirrar

Duck

Quack

Quak

Pato

Cow

Moo

Mu

24 Vaca

Phone

Ring

Trimm

Telefone

Monkey

Ooh-ooh-ahh-ahh

u-u-ááá

Macaco

Frog

Ribbit

Croac

Rã

Hush

Shh

chi

Silêncio

Rooster

Cock-a-doodle-doo

Cocorocó

Galo

Drums

Boom

Boom

Bateria

Snake

Hiss

Sssssss

Serpente

Owl

Hoot

U-huu

Coruja

Bee

BUZZ

BZZZZZZ

Abelha

Hands

Clap

Palakpak

Mãos

Lamb

Baa

Beee

Cordeiro 27

Crawl

Rastejar

Roll
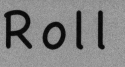

Rolar

Walk

Andar

28

Run

Correr

Hop

Pular

Ride

Andar de bicicleta

Kiss

Beijar

Jump

Saltar

29

Happy

Sad

Feliz

Triste

Angry

Scared

30 Zangada

Assustada

Frustration

Frustração

Surprise

Surpresa

Shock

Choque

Brave

Corajosa 31

Baseball

Basebol

Basketball

Basquetebol

Tennis

Tênis

Soccer

Futebol

Badminton

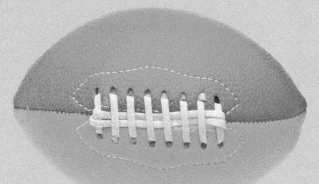

Badminton

Football

Futebol americano

Volleyball

Voleibol

Golf

Golfe

33

Fire truck

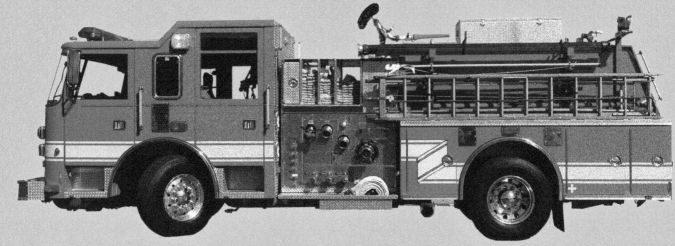

Caminhão de bombeiros

Car

Truck

34 Carro

Caminhão

Helicopter

Helicóptero

Airplane

Avião

Train

Trem

Boat

Barco

35

Small   Medium   Large

Pequeno Médio Grande

Small   Medium   Large

36 Pequeno   Médio   Grande

Large   Medium   Small

Grande   Médio   Pequeno

Large   Medium   Small

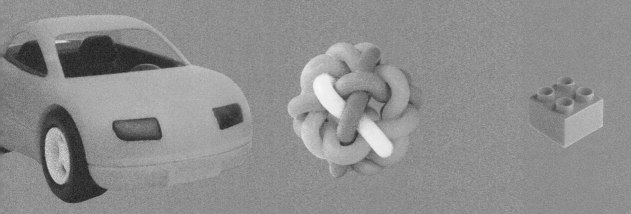

Grande   Médio   Pequeno 37

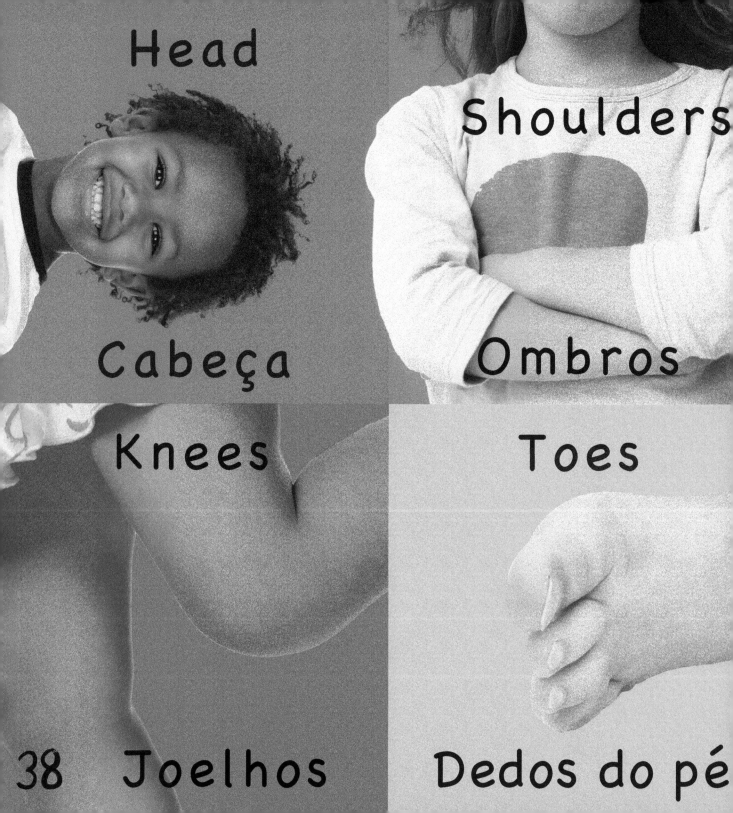

Head
Cabeça

Shoulders
Ombros

Knees
Toes

38 Joelhos

Dedos do pé

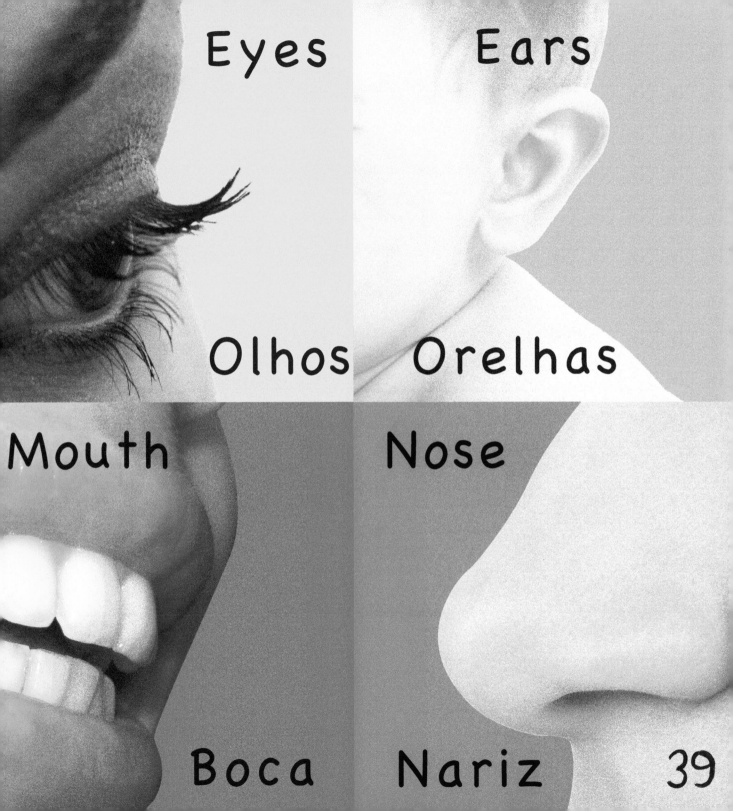

Eyes

Ears

Olhos

Orelhas

Mouth

Nose

Boca

Nariz

39

Sippy cup

Copo com canudinho

Bowl

Tigela

Pot

40 Panela

Cup

Copo

Plate	Fork
Prato	Garfo
Knife	Spoon
Faca	Colher 41

Hat

Chapéu

Shirt

Camiseta

Pants

Calça

Shorts

Calção

Gloves

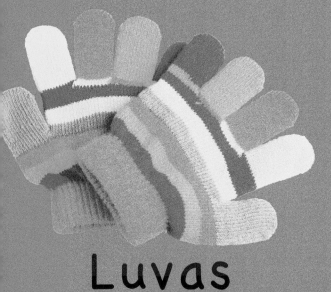

Luvas

Sunglasses

Óculos de sol

Socks

Meias

Shoes

Sapatos 43

Bath time
Hora do banho

Bath

Banheira

Soap

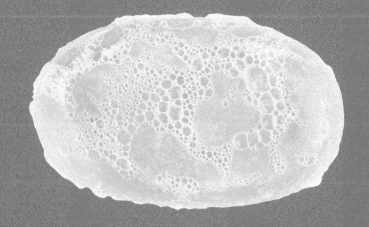

44 Sabonete

Towel

Toalha

Brush

Escovar os dentes

Book

Livro

Potty

Bacio

Bed

Cama

45

THE T❤DDLER'S HANDB❤❤K

Match the following to the pictures below. Can you find **7 pumpkins, a hooting owl, a rainbow, a baseball, a lion, square blocks, a sad boy, a helicopter, and shoes?**

Faça o seguinte para as imagens abaixo. Você consegue encontrar **7 abóboras, uma coruja, um arco-íris, uma bola de basebol, um leão, blocos quadrados, um menino triste, um helicóptero e sapatos?**

helicopter / helicóptero

shoes / sapatos

hooting owl / coruja

baseball / bola de basebol

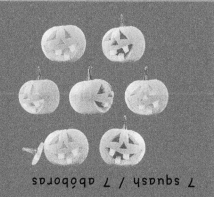

7 squash / 7 abóboras

boy / menino triste

lion / leão

square blocks / blocos quadrados

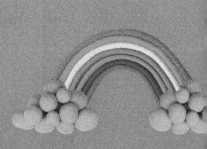

rainbow / arco-íris

46